MACDONALD STARTERS

D1395484

Dinosaurs

Macdonald Educational

About Macdonald Starters

Macdonald Starters are vocabulary controlled information books for young children. More than ninety per cent of the words in the text will be in the reading vocabulary of the vast majority of young readers. Word and sentence length have also been carefully controlled.

Key new words associated with the topic of each book are repeated with picture explanations in the Starters dictionary at the end. The dictionary can also be used as an index for teaching children to look things up.

Teachers and experts have been consulted on the content and accuracy of the books.

Illustrated by: Laurent Sauveur Sant

Editors: Peter Usborne, Su Swallow

Reading consultant: Donald Moyle, author of *The Teaching of Reading* and senior lecturer in education at Edge Hill College of Education

Chairman, teacher advisory panel: F. F. Blackwell, general inspector for schools, London Borough of Croydon, with responsibility for primary education

Teacher panel: Elizabeth Wray, Loveday Harmer, Lynda Snowdon, Joy West

This is a dinosaur's skeleton.
Dinosaurs lived long, long ago.

Long ago the world looked different.
There were no people.
The plants were different.
2

The animals were different.
Some of the animals were dinosaurs.
There were different kinds of dinosaurs.

3

Some dinosaurs were small.
This one ate other animals.
It was a meat eater.
4

This dinosaur was very big.
It was a plant eater.
It walked on four legs.

The big dinosaur was very heavy.
Sometimes it stood in the water.
The water helped it to stand.

This dinosaur ate plants.
It had spikes on its tail.
The spikes helped it fight.

This dinosaur had a bony collar on
its neck.
It also had horns on its head.
These helped to keep it safe.

8

This dinosaur was very tall.
It walked on two legs.
It ate other dinosaurs.

The tall dinosaur had a big head.
It had lots of sharp teeth.

This dinosaur ate plants and trees.
It stood on its back legs.
Each foot had three toes.

There were other animals too.
They were not dinosaurs.
Some flew in the air.
12

Some swam in the water.

This dinosaur died by a lake.
It fell down in the mud.
14

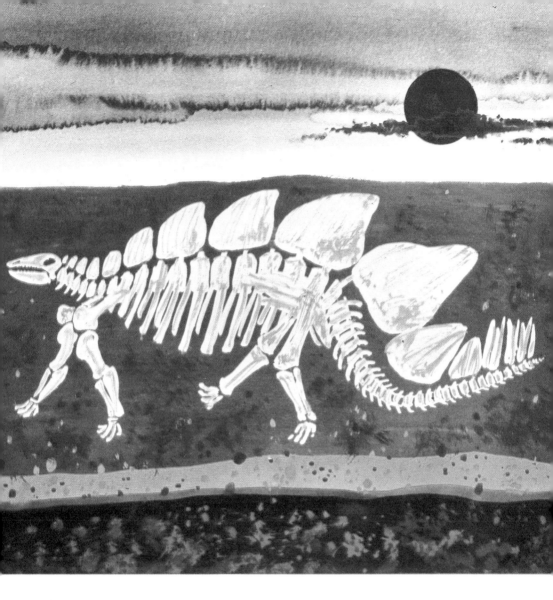

It became a skeleton.
After a long time,
the mud covered the bones.

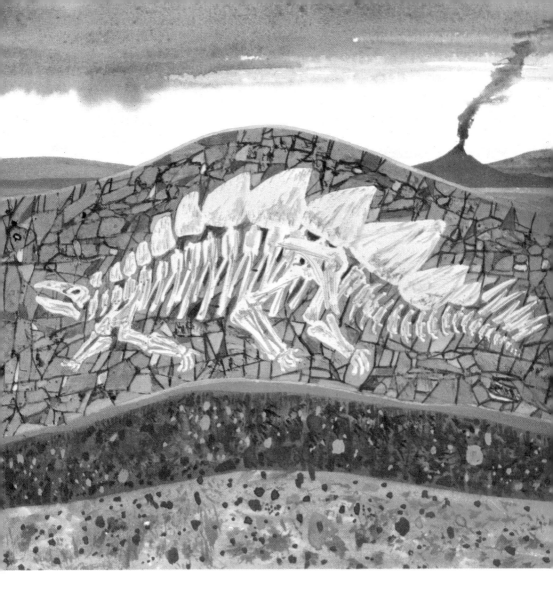

The mud slowly turned into rock.
The bones turned into fossils.
16

After a long time,
the rocks were pushed up.
The fossils came to the top again.

Scientists look for fossils in rocks.
They found the fossil dinosaur bones.
They took the fossil bones from the rocks.
18

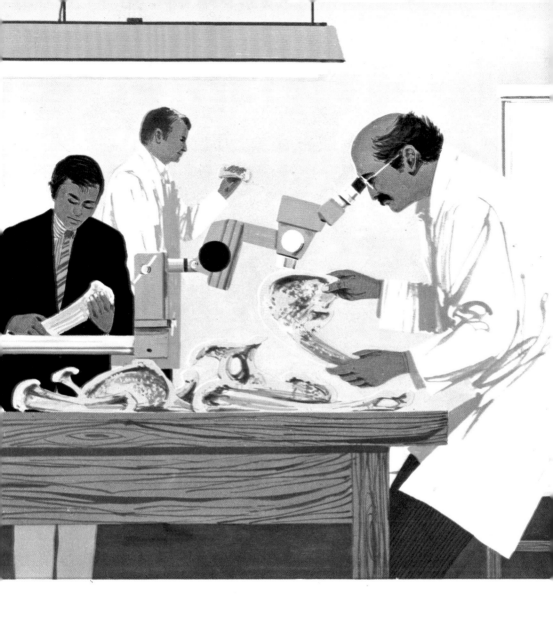

They took the fossil bones to the museum.
They put the bones together.

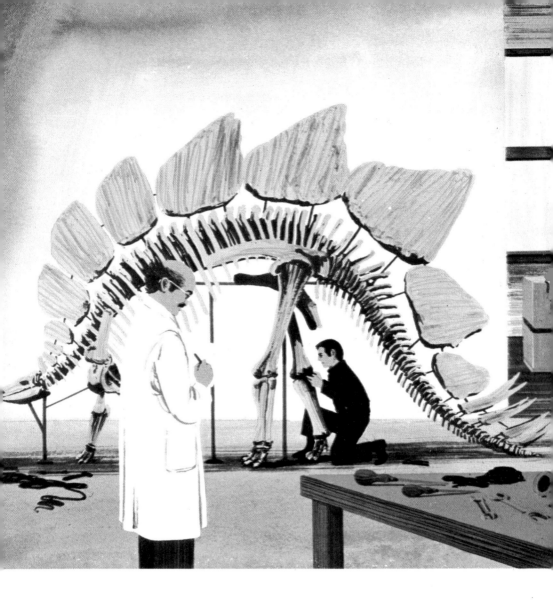

The scientist made the skeleton again.
It shows the shape of the dinosaur.
20

Then a man painted a picture.
It shows what the dinosaur looked like.

Diplodocus

Compsognathus

Triceratops

Iguanodon

Tyrannosaurus

Stegosaurus

See for yourself.

Here are the names of the dinosaurs in this book.

Try to read them.

Try to find them in a museum.

22

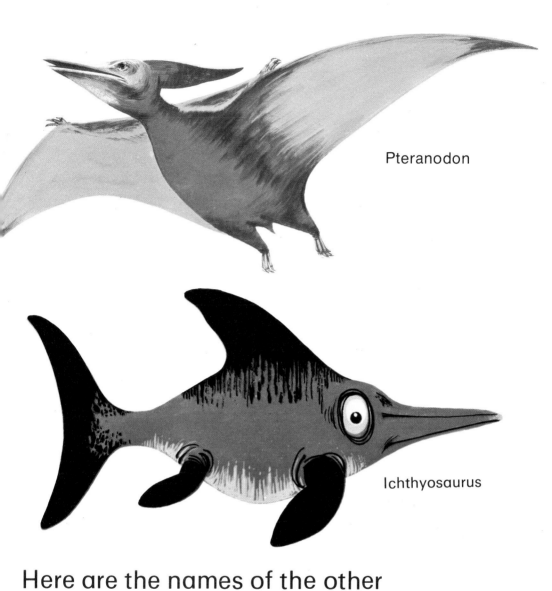

Pteranodon

Ichthyosaurus

Here are the names of the other
animals in the book.
They lived at the time of the dinosaurs.
Try to read them.

Starter's **Dinosaurs** words

skeleton
(page 1)

toe
(page 11)

spike
(page 7)

bone
(page 15)
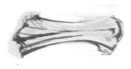

bony collar
(page 8)

fossil
(page 16)

horn
(page 8)

scientist
(page 18)

back legs
(page 11)

museum
(page 19)

24